WALKING IN IT

MELISSA L. LEE

Copyright © 2022 Bondage Breakthrough Blessings All rights reserved

The characters and events portrayed in this book are real. And similarity to real people, living or dead, is coincidental and not intended by the author.

No part of this book may be reproduced, or stored in a retrieval system, or transmitted in any form or by any means, electronic, mechanical, photocopying, recording, or otherwise, without express written permission of the publisher.

ISBN-13: 979-8-9861062-0-5

Cover design by: Chris Lee
Library of Congress Control Number: 2018675309
Printed in the United States of America

BONDAGE BREAKTHROUGH BLESSINGS

DEDICATED TO

MY MOTHER

JOYCE MARIE JENKINS

MY HUSBAND CHRIS ANTHONY LEE

MY CHILDREN DEJA K. JENKINS NIA HARRIS MAKAYLA LANIER

BONDAGE BREAKTHROUGH BLESSINGS

CONTENTS

1	I'm Coming Out	Pg 11-19
2	Baby Steps	Pg 20-28
3	Turning Point	Pg 29-35
4	The Progression	Pg 36-44
5	My Purpose	Pg 45-54
6	Claiming My Calling	Pg 55-64
7	Pick Me Up	Pg 65-73
8	Hibernation	Pg 74-80
9	Self-Deception	Pg 81-89
10	Victory Is Mine	Pg 90-101
11	Breakthrough	Pg 102-110
12	Moving On	Pg 111-118
13	Different Faces	Pg 119-126
14	It's Not About You Or Me	Pg 127-136

15	Better Days Are Coming	Pg137-146
16	Faith Avenue	Pg147-155
17	Trust Fall	Pg156-164
18	Staying Grounded	Pg165-172
19	My God My Mechanic	Pg173-181
20	Stir The Word In You	Pg182-189
21	Layers Removed	Pg190-198
22	Make Me, Mold Me	Pg199-205
23	Keeping The Enemy Away	Pg206-214

Behind every situation there is a story
Behind every story there was a process
Behind every process there was some Pain
Behind all the pain there is purpose
Never let your pain be greater than your purpose

MELISSA LAKEYIA LEE

**OWN IT
LIVE IT
ACCEPT IT
ACKNOWLEDGE IT....
BUT WHATEVER YOU
DO
DONT STOP WALKING
IN IT**

Isaiah 43:1-2

But now thus saith the LORD that created thee, O Jacob, and he that formed thee, O Israel, Fear not: for I have redeemed thee, I have called *thee* by thy name; thou *art* mine. When thou passest through the waters, I *will be* with thee; and through the rivers, they shall not overflow thee: when thou walkest through the fire, thou shalt not be burned; neither shall the flame kindle upon thee.

CHAPTER ONE

I'M COMING OUT

I cannot continue to walk the way I have done before. I have spent so much time walking as if I was being pushed to walk. I was a zombie literally walking in my pain and every day, hoping that I would soon rise up and walk in what the Lord had for me, despite all that I was carrying.

A few months had passed on, and I felt everything. I did not want that feeling of emptiness to come back to me, and I refused to go back and forth to a place that I promised myself I would never go back to again. When

I was coming out, I promised myself that I would walk all the way, no matter how long it took me.

There is a saying that "You have to crawl before you walk." Yes, this was one of those situations. Even though I had come through it all, I still revisit them at times, but I will not walk in the mud and get stuck this time around. I know there is greater coming out of the pain that I have endured.

I found myself waking up after the Lord had revealed such greatness to me, reminding me that no matter how bad it gets today, I will push through. I placed my feet on the floor and would sit for a while, telling myself that this would be a good day, despite what my mind was telling me. The mindset plays a big part in your growth, and if the mind is not connected to your heart, then there is no way to defeat the opposing side.

While going through my toughest battles, I learned that if your mind is not lined up and filled with positive thoughts, then there is no way to bind it and remove it from your life. It takes courage to get rid of the negative thoughts. So, I decided to take the trash out and move on from anything that would stop me from personally growing in the Lord, despite the tears it caused me to shed.

"Your choice: You can come out or stay in, but you will not see a change hiding behind any door."

When you are coming out of a storm or are going through your storm, it is absolutely imperative to keep your mindset upon greatness, and I am speaking about the Lord. Tragedy will show that you sometimes have to be okay with stepping out and staying out. There can be no more hiding behind the trees or sitting in the furthest corner, no more running or putting on the blinders.

Even in your smallest steps of recovery, every move that you make is important. The wrong turn may cause great damage to your foundation. Lay the concrete, stand on it, and begin to walk in it.

I do know that any pain will cause a person to break down completely, but any amount of rehabilitation should allow you to stand up in it. The heartache from loved ones being caught up in the clouds unexpectedly can certainly shift your whole world, as it did mine. However, you can either wallow in your pain, or you can walk in it. I choose to walk in it.

Walking in your pain is not as simple as it sounds, and I know some can agree. It always seemed easier to give up than to take up your cross. However, I failed to realize that I didn't have to. It was not my battle. It was the Lord's. I did struggle with this from time to time. How could I just expect the Lord to carry my burden, even though the Word tells us to cast our burdens on the Lord?

I had become impatient, thinking that a miracle would just happen overnight.

I had to be willing to walk, and not only walk, but walk in whatever I had been through, carried, and lost. I no longer wanted to continue to attend the same "sorrowful service" in my mind over and over again. It became repetitive, and something needed to be done. The crutch that was holding me up had to be loosened. I did not want to be restricted anymore to my own pain.

There are two options when you are dealing with situations such as the ones I had been dealt. Either you will remain stuck, or you will start to pick up your feet and walk. I chose to walk. I have found that through this walk, I have had to stop and take some small breaks in between, just enough to gather myself and keep going.

I sat in the car one day in the middle of having a breakdown, and the Lord placed me right where He wanted me to be at that time.

I sat across from a house where a man was up on a ladder. He climbed the ladder to get to the roof, and I noticed that he did not look down at every step. I took that as the Lord revealing something to me.

The Lord was telling me to keep

climbing, let Him guide, and not look down. He was not always steady, and the ladder shook from time to time. I was praying as he was climbing up the ladder, saying, "Lord, please keep him, cover him, and protect him on his climb." He safely made it to the top.

When he got off of the ladder, I saw that he sighed with relief. While he was on the ladder, he did not look down. I am sure he thought about this process and the fear of falling. I did not see anyone around him or the house.

It was just him and GOD. I then had to think about it for myself. There may be up to five people around, or no one around when I go anywhere or do anything, and the Lord will always be present. I can only imagine the fear that came over this man as he was climbing the ladder. He obviously was very determined to get to the top to complete his task, which is how we must think.

We have to ask the Lord to carry us over every mountain we believe may be a barrier. There is no one bigger than the GOD that we serve. If you have tried every obstacle and you find yourself right back where you started, then maybe you should try GOD. He is our only answer in all situations.

Psalm 32:8

I will instruct thee and teach thee in the way which thou shalt go: I will guide thee with mine eye.

CHAPTER *TWO*
BABY STEPS

I have had these days where I had to look back and evaluate my purpose, my pain, and my time to praise through everything that I have been through. I lost myself down many of the roads that I had to conquer. I realized that after all of the pitfalls I had fallen into.

It was then that I realized that even though I had experienced many pitfalls. I needed to backtrack and remember everything that I had already accomplished in my life. After the tragedy I had been through, I just could not figure out how to pick myself back up. It all started when I felt like I could not get back into a stable environment, starting with what I did on an everyday basis, which was work.

I had become comfortable with what I was doing, and I was stagnant about even moving ahead in life. I became so comfortable when a crisis had hit my life, that I could in no way pick myself back up and start over.

My associates told me that it was okay, "You just need to slow down," but that must have been the worst thing that I could have done. My grandfather always used to say if I stop working it will kill me. I felt the same way in some aspects of my life. I gave up and used the excuse that because I had experienced such a tragedy, I could not function.

Some people can clearly say that taking a break is or was good for them after taking such a big loss. However, that did not work for me; I had to get back to me. I owed that to myself. I had to start somewhere, no matter what anyone had thought. It was my sanity that I needed to keep. I had to find the broken pieces and put them back together again.

"Sometimes you have to get back down and crawl all over again."

The leaves that were starting to wither away needed to be revived. The breaths I took had even become shallow. I had to tell myself over and over on plenty of occasions that I am not just existing; I am living. I do not know if people are aware of the difference, but there is a difference.

I was waking up every day doing the same routine. It takes the person themself to understand they are living in a bubble. The only way that you get in that position is if you put yourself there. The only way to be released from that world is if you release yourself from it.

I had many people praying for me, and I knew the Lord could heal me and He did. However, I had to not only accept the healing, but also believe that I was released from the entrapment of my own pain.

I am breathing, I am released. I am Living. If it takes baby steps to get you back to where you need to be, then that is fine. We all must start somewhere. There is a saying that says, "We have to crawl before we walk," and in this case, that is what I had to do to build myself back up to walk.

Some days, I even felt as if I was physically impaired and unable to stand, looking for a chair to pull up and sit on. I will tell you this, as long as there is a crutch there to hold you up, you may not ever be able to walk. So, I will say to you, get up and walk, move ahead, look up, and do not look down. GOD has you.

There were times through my storms when I felt like I was walking on a balance beam, unsteady, and ready to fall off again at any time, but I did not give up.

I made a mental statement to myself that if I have to start from the beginning and recap everything, then that is what I will do. There have been many people who I have crossed paths with and come back in contact with.

A few questions that always came up was "So what are you doing with yourself now?" Considering that I had to backtrack my life and take *small steps, I would just reply and say, "Well you know some things had occurred, not trying to go back and pick at my wounds." Then the next question would be, "So what happened?" Again, my next response would be, "A lot, but **GOD**…"*

*No matter how many stops, breaks, or replays you may have to do, just don't give up. **GOD** is always on the throne. Baby steps are better than no steps at all. A slow pace is better than no pace at all, considering that we serve a **GOD** that is always available.*

No matter how slow you go you must move out of your tunnel, just move! There is greatness waiting for you. Do not focus on what it looks like. Think about what it will be like once you get through.

When a baby starts crawling, you

will see them move very slowly, then they pick up their pace, and eventually, they will begin to pull themselves up and walk around the edge of the couch or table, then they let go and start moving on their own.

Do you see the steps you are taking? After you begin to walk again, then you can begin to run. Whether you crawl, walk, or run, don't stop. There is a reward.

I believe that if you can crawl, you can walk, and if you can walk, then you can get exactly where you are going. I have never seen a baby take off running straight out of the womb, so it is absolutely okay to move at the pace the Lord has set for you. I think when we move too fast (or faster than we should), it could be a major setback.

Have you ever seen a track field? I

am sure that you have. Do you think about how far it looks if you are barely moving? I would rather complete it barely moving than not moving at all. It feels so good to look back and see all the ground you have covered when you thought that you could not cover any bit of any road. Every step counts.

A little progress while grieving is a major process when you are surrounded by negative energy, while also looking back on where you used to be before life happened. I urge you to stay in the race.

**Philippians 4
And I intreat thee also, true yokefellow, help those women which laboured with me in the gospel, with Clement also, and with other my fellowlabourers, whose names are in the book of life.**

CHAPTER THREE
Turning Point

The day had come to make a difference; it had to be done. No more procrastination, and no more setbacks on my part. I felt that I was in a position where I was dealing with my biggest setback.

I would plan to start my day, and it would almost seem like my feet were stuck in mud. I literally could not move my feet. I said to myself, "This is not what your family would want for you to do, no matter how bad this pain feels, you have to move on."

I would have many conversations with myself saying "It is time to move on." I had given a mini sermon in church one Sunday, and I never speak about anything that I have been through. So, the question is, "Move on from what?"

The main thing that I needed to move on from was depression. It was depression that kept me tied down. It was the anger and the bitterness on the inside that I was not able to shake. It was in me, and I needed to shake it loose. I was at a point in my life where I started accepting that depression was just a part of my life and that it was never going to go away.

Proverbs 13:3 speaks about this. It states, "He that keepeth his mouth keepeth his life: but he that openeth wide his lips shall have destruction." I was bringing destruction into my own life. People would ask me how I was doing, and I would respond by saying, "I am depressed," as if I was in a stable condition.

I had already put myself in critical condition, literally ready to be put on life support. I was sucking my own energy out of my life. The devil convinced me he could pull the plug on me at any given second. He was using me as his personal assistant by allowing this daunting darkness to hover over me for way too long.

I had to pause for a moment. It was time and the time was overdue. A change had to come, and it was up to me to make the change and stick to it.

"Make a decision and turn the wheel."

This part of my life was called a turning point. Something had to change, and it needed to be permanent. No more dwelling on the falling tears and the pain within. This clock is moving on and I have to catch up. I would lay there knowing that I had an opportunity to change. However, I would let depression override me, knowing that I literally had to turn some things around for the better of me. At this point, what did "For the better of me" mean?

There was much buried, and I needed it to come out. I needed to get the dirt off me, rise and turn my situation around. I knew I had the Lord there to guide me through, as he already was doing. It took me accepting that my life needed to flip back, and that I needed to revert to who I knew I was, who I could be, and who I needed to be.

I had to do this not only for myself, but also for my family, and most of all for the Lord.

I could not be effective in my ministry if I could not change the way I was thinking or my actions. I found myself demonstrating nonchalant behavior and caring for nothing. Nothing seemed to make me happy, which is not of GOD. As people regardless of religious beliefs, every day is a blessing, a chance to make a change, and do something great in the Lord. This part of my life is called "the Turning Point."

A turning point simply indicates a change either for the better or for the worse. In this case, it had to be for the better. It was necessary for this to happen. I know everything that I was presented with has shaped, formed, and made me who I am today.

Sometimes we go through storms never understanding the reasons. There are also some things we will never understand or be able to comprehend. While waiting for a possible answer, there is no need to stay in one mindset when change is needed. I am a firm believer that the Lord wants all his children to prosper and be full of happiness.

I believe He is and already has turned it around for me. There is no such thing as the Lord only giving you just a little bit when he wants you to have it all. He will do a complete 360 on your life if you let Him. There is nothing partial about a change from the Lord.

Philippians 3:13-14

Brethren, I count not myself to have apprehended: but this one thing I do, forgetting those things which are behind, and reaching forth unto those things which are before, I press toward the mark for the prize of the high calling of God in Christ Jesus.

CHAPTER FOUR
The Progression

I am at the point of progression. Everyone knows that progression means to move forth, let those things behind you be. It doesn't necessarily mean to forget, but to push past. The hurt, the pain, and the anguish. Many days I had to look to my Bible, my phone, or those sticky notes that said, "You have to push through this, you have come through the worst parts of it all."

As I now look back now, I see the pain that I endured, the tears that I had to fight back, and the times where I had to position myself to deal with the backlash that came with everything that had taken place in my life over the last two years. My character is being tested; my faith is being weighed. Every move that I make from this point on will determine who I am beyond all the trauma that has taken place.

At times, I believed that people would try to push me to see how far they could take me. I believe that they did this to see if I would leave my Christianity behind or as some say, put it to the side. I will always carry the same scripture with me after coming out of so much turmoil. The scripture in Psalms 119:11 states, "Thy word I have hidden in my heart, that I might not sin against thee."

Yes, I carried my Lord in my pocket, my heart, my mind, and everywhere I go. I know that as I pass through every chapter of my life that the GOD that I serve cradled me the whole way through. I am His, just like you are His. I would tell anyone to cast your cares upon the Lord because He will see you through it all.

"Progress is everything, even if it's a little at a time."

During the process of progression, what I can share with anyone is that you will not be able to move ahead without first realizing where your help comes from. My Source is the Lord. When it comes to progression in any situation, you must first understand that sometimes even self-help is not always enough.

I found myself thinking that I could help myself and avoid other outside sources. Beside the help of my Lord, you can surround yourself with Christ-like people, and positivity.

You have to learn to speak life into yourself. That is what I did. I found myself talking to myself quite often and encouraging myself. You cannot expect others to build you up and root for you if you will not do it for yourself. Some people will prey on your downfall of progression, while other people will pray for your progression. They don't mix, it's like vinegar and oil.

I would have some people reach out to me and speak life into me, while others seemed to want me to just lay down and die. I knew better than to feed into that. I knew (and know) that my life still had a purpose, and that I needed to fulfill my goals in this life that was given to me. I could have been cut off in so many ways, but I was not.

The Lord saw purpose in me, and I will give my all to deliver what he has instilled in me from birth. Everything that is on the inside can possibly grow, it just has to be delivered in some form. I want to be delivered from anything that will set me apart from what the Lord has for me. There is a song, and the lyrics say, "What God has for me it is for me."

I believe that underneath all the pain and anguish that I carried for some time, that after all that is uncovered and no longer buried, that then I can rise up and move ahead.

I have never been to a funeral service twice. So, if you have been in similar situations, no matter what it is, I am asking you to join with me and move around, no longer allowing yourself to revisit the same service. I am still here with a purpose and if you are reading this book, so are you.

I have been sleeping long enough and it is time for me to wake up. I was always told that the clock does not stop for anyone. I don't want to look back anymore and see that time was wasted.

I think over and over about a dream I had. There was one road headed up and once you got to the end of the road, you could make a left or right turn. The first time I got to the light, I turned left and ended up back on the same road going forward. The second time that I got to the top of the road I made a left. Guess what? I ended up on the same road.

The third time, I drove up the road and instead of turning left or right, I decided to keep going ahead. The Lord had revealed to me that neither right nor left was correct, and to move ahead was my only option.

Life will take you on some turns, flips, and have you all over the place.

The only true direction for any progression in your life is our great GOD. He is the author, the finisher, the mediator, my counselor, and most of all, the compass of my life.

I promise you if you are lost or you feel yourself getting lost, seek guidance and direction from GOD. Many people will try to tell you that you should have done this, and you should have done that, but I can assure you there is only one true advisor; he is our Lord and Savior.

A lot of times during my transition of healing, I did not seek people, because in some cases, you may think that you could be telling someone the right thing, but later realize that what you told them only created a deeper hole for them.

There is a medication that does not have an expiration date, and there is no such thing as an overdose. It is called the WORD. Let the words of the Bible lead you in any direction.

There is no progression in circles. Let's keep moving forward together, but also be prepared to move forward alone if that is what needs to be done.

Psalm 57:2

I will cry unto God most high; Unto God that performeth all things for me.

CHAPTER FIVE
My purpose

My purpose has been identified. I went through one of the biggest storms in life that I would not wish on anyone. I had been going through off and on in my Christian walk like most people. I was in and out, still having doubts that I could even carry on the assignment that was previously placed on my life.

When the Lord speaks to your heart, it can make you nervous, and I heard one person say they felt like they wanted to run from themself. I get it. I do. In the midst of the inevitable, I was just getting myself in a certain place with the Lord.

I was moving ahead, then my life

took a turn, but in the midst of it all, there was still a calling, a job, an assignment that had to be carried out.

I had experienced some things prior to the passing of my loved ones, and the Lord had given me a glance at both heaven and hell. He spared me once again. He gave me a second chance.

The way I had looked at it is that a choice needed to be made and it needed to be made as soon as possible. Even though I had gone through so many things in two years, I still had to carry out what was placed on me. So, "What did that mean for me?" was the question that came up in my life.

There had to be a complete change. My life needed to be lined up and my walk needed to go straight forward, not sideways, and not in between.

I will say to you that if you are assigned a task from the Lord, either you will accept it or you won't. I can tell you this: if you are running from your purpose, you will (like myself) find yourself going in circles, back and forth, finding yourself right back at point A. "Lord, I hear you loud and clear," are the words I had spoken into the atmosphere.

"Each individual has to pursue their purpose."

I then knew no matter what I came against in this life, I had to accept it and understand that it is His will and there is no wrong when it comes to the GOD that I serve.

Through the heartaches, the pain, and the many days I wanted to lay down and let it all go, there still was no room in me for what I wanted, but what the Lord desired of me to do. Have you ever been in the midst of doing something around the house and suddenly words are spoken to your heart? That is what happened to me through my struggles with depression.

I was upstairs in my room folding my clothes. I began to get very emotional, and I did not know why. I heard the Lord speak these words to me. He said, "You can run from Me but you cannot hide from Me," and I replied back and said, "Okay Lord, I was one of your chosen ones, so I will do Your will."

When this occurred, I sat down on the bed and began to praise Him over and over again.

You can have the best job in the world, or think you have the best job in the world, but until you are a worker, follower, and servant of the Lord, you have not yet received the best Occupation yet, Praise God! My assignment is mandatory. I could have been called home years ago, but He still has work for me to do.

If you have wondered what your purpose is, pray, seek, and wait to hear. The Lord may show you through demonstration. He may show you by speaking to your heart. Just be ready to receive the great news, yes I said great news.

When I look back on my life, I can actually say to myself "The Lord has been so good to me, despite the heartache and the pain." I know now what I need to do to live the life the Lord has designed for me.

I will ask you the same question. What is it that GOD has for you? There is no servant bigger than the other. We all serve a great purpose. I hope to see you there with me when we all fulfill our work in the Lord.

There is a song that says, "What GOD has for me, it is for me." I will tell you the same. "What GOD has for you, it is for you." We all have a great purpose here on this earth. No one is here without a true calling. Grab your purpose and run with it.

The scripture of Jeremiah 29:11 states, "For I know the plans I have for you, declares the LORD, plans to prosper you and not to harm you, plans to give you hope and a future." This is clear, the Lord does not hold any great thing from you. There is work to be done. Let us reach for greater. Greater is coming. We were all bought for a price and for a purpose.

My service unto the Lord is mandatory, nothing less. I owe him that much. Since we all have a purpose, I will say that it is time for all of us to begin seeking the Lord and finding out our purpose. There is a book out called "Purpose Driven Life." There is purpose in everything that occurs in our lives.

I have always had a love for the Lord, and prior to my life changing I was still asking the Lord from time to time, "What is it exactly that you have for me to do?"

I do know that He wanted me to work in the area of helping others. I was just not sure exactly how I would be helping others. This all came with time. I never knew that I would be helping other women, mothers, and even young women who were grieving and going through hard times in life.

I had gone back to a ministry that I had come up with in 2017 called Bondage, Breakthrough and Blessing. Here it is 2021, and I am just now starting to build on it. When I speak to people about my ministry, I always let them know that this did not come to me overnight.

It had been years that had passed before I really understood why the Lord was directing me on this path. It took many years of praying and asking GOD exactly what my assignment was.

Sometimes we get tired of praying and think that the LORD does not hear us. Guess what? He really does. I had come to the conclusion that if He didn't answer my prayers in a certain time frame, then it was for a good reason. The Lord will sometimes block certain things in our lives because He may feel that right now is just not the right time.

I am also a firm believer that when every prayer request comes to the Lord, He will want you to be in a certain place in your life so you can initiate His plan for your life. We all know that there are no half steps with the Lord.

Either you are in, or you are out. Which one are you? Do you know your purpose? If not, keep seeking. I assure you, with time you will know. There is no assignment that the Lord will keep from you. He wants us all to fulfill our purpose.

Ephesians 2:10

For we are his workmanship, created in Christ Jesus unto good works, which God hath before ordained that we should walk in them.

CHAPTER *SIX*
Claiming My Calling

I am in acceptance. I have received the calling of my life. Since I had accepted what I needed to do to be on the walk with my Lord, everything seemed to be a little bit clearer to me. Why did it take this long to get it?

I felt at times that I was playing tug-of-war with my own mind, going back and forth with what was to be. There would be plenty of nights that I would wake up and sit on the side of the bed after the Lord had shown me in my sleep exactly what I would be doing.

He showed me in a large building filled with people praising the Lord. I was speaking in that dream.

I was touching many hearts, as well as my own. I found that what was in me to minister to other people was also ministering to myself. It seemed so real. I did not know anyone there but that is okay, we are all GOD'S people. We all belong to Him.

I noticed that I was standing at the podium where I had questioned myself plenty of times before. It was in my own church where our pastors allowed us to grow and speak the word of GOD.

I knew then that what I was running from was an assignment that was in the book of my life. I'm claiming it at this point. I would find myself at work, in the community, or even at the local store speaking with people about how good God is, and how we cannot make it in this world without Him.

Some people came to me with the particular question of, "How do you know that you were called to do the Lord's work?" My response was "Well, the Lord spoke to my heart."

He has shown me in dreams, and I just know. However, you will also know because we were all put on this earth to do something, both big and small.

I taught my Sunday class one time about their purpose here, and I explained to them that everyone has requirements that they need to fulfill before their time is up. One of the students said, "Well, how will I know my purpose?" I said, "He will let you know. Just pray, seek and He will let you know."

I shared with them that I had seen a man walking down the street and he was full of alcohol on certain days. I would see him, not knowing if he was in the same condition. However, he did something that was very Christian like.

He saw an older woman struggling with her groceries as she was trying to get into her home.
As I saw him approaching her, I started instantly praying from my kitchen window.

I was praying that he would help her and not hurt her. He took each one of her bags to her door and kindly walked away. I heard her telling him, "Come back, I will pay you."
The man raised his hands up and said "These hands were made for helping."

While helping her, he may have found his calling. Days following, I would see him more and more. He then started working in her yard, again, with no pay. "This is the Lord's work," he explained to the older lady.

"Either sign the line or move on."

I had gone across the street to speak to her. We talked off and on throughout the week about the neighborhood in general. She said, "I don't know where he comes from, but it was definitely on time."

See, the Lord will use who He wants when He wants, and for what He wants. It turns out she did not have any family. She passed away about a year later and she left the house to him. He started his own family with that home.

The reason I am sharing this story is to say that his very purpose may have been fulfilled at that time in his life.

We all have a purpose, and Romans 8:28 (KJV) states, "And we know that all things work together for good to them that love God, to them who are called according to His purpose."

So, regardless of what he had been through, his purpose could have been to help her through her last year on this earth. No matter what your calling is, big or small, let it be of GOD. I promise you that He will direct your paths. If He, did it for me, He will do it for you.

I have even questioned whether I am even worthy enough for Him to bless me in such a way as He has done.

Why should He not bless me, though?

I am His and He always wants His children to be blessed. I think many of us struggle with the fact that we are not good enough to be blessed. It is a mindset that we adopt from the world. It is in His Word that the Lord takes care of His own.

Allow the Lord to take care of you, lead you, and listen for your calling; we all have one. Once you know that you have a purpose, you then will accept that you are called.

Only you will know the call on your life. No one can know that before you. Your pastor or a prophet may speak things into your life and see what the Lord has shown them, but it is ultimately up to you to follow through.

You will have people who will look at your past, no matter what you have been through, and will judge you based on it. They will not understand how you are in the position that you are currently in.

You can certainly say, in a nice way, to look up the scripture of Romans 8:30, which states, "Moreover whom he predestined, them he also called; and whom he called, then he also justified, and whom he justified, them he also glorified."

Many of us do not feel that we are called. We do not feel worthy of anything or to even be a worker of the Lord for whatever reason. However, He loves us all the same and He knew who we were before we came into the world.

He already had everything set

up for us in the time and way that He saw fit. I am writing this and saying to myself, "Thank you Lord." I did not start living until I started living for the Lord. People will assume that just because you are a Christian that your life is boring. I will say this loud and clear.

Now that I am Living for the Lord, I am living my best life because although I am suffering, I will tell you, the Lord has my back, my front, and my side. I can be blindfolded, but the Lord still has been present. He did not bring me this far to let me go.

Exodus 15:2

The LORD is my strength and song, And he is become my salvation: He is my God, and I will prepare him an habitation; My father's God, and I will exalt him.

CHAPTER *SEVEN*
Pick Me Up

So, as you know, when we walk with Christ, and you have accepted your calling, the devil gets really busy. He tends to pull on you like never before.

When you are not living your life according to God's will, you can rest assured that the devil is not going to bother you, since he has you in his court.

I felt like as long as I was claiming and walking in my depression and having a carnal mindset, that the devil did not bother me at all. If you think about it, the devil did not have to bother me because I was walking around with his demeanor, but as soon as I claimed my walk, everything that could come up against me did.

The devil had already tried to take me out with my family being gone, but even with that, there are days where I have to remind myself of what the Word says.

The devil cannot do anything that the Lord does not allow. He seemed to do what he needed to do at that time. I was on a good path and looked at what happened to the devil, who tried me in every angle that he could.

One of the sermons that I used was that I was touched, but it did not affect me. When we receive and accept our calling, we must understand that all kinds of things will come against us. We will fall, we will have our faults, we will come short of the Glory, but just don't make it a habit.

I have heard people say, "Well, He is a forgiving GOD, so if I fall short, he will forgive me." Focus on asking the Lord to pick you up when you fall short of His expectations. If you can say that your life is perfect and every angle of it is well, then you might be doing something wrong.

"We all need a lift sometimes."

The devil has a plan for all of our downfalls, and he preys on our weaknesses. One of my favorite books in the Bible is the book of Job. I called myself having "the case of the jobs." Yes, I was attacked in so many areas after I accepted my walk with Christ.

I can honestly say I was being obedient in my assignment, but not of true acceptance. I will tell you this, one of the things that I have experienced is that when my mind was made up, I believe that the devil received a message regarding me and here came all the attacks: the finances, the sickness, my children and so forth, but nothing was greater than my desire to please the Lord.

When I had the desire to please a man and the world, I did not have a worry in the world. There is a saying that all good things come to an end, but with the LORD everything is everlasting.

It does not get any better than that. Each and every time that I felt that the devil was trying to attack me, I would say, "LORD PICK ME UP," and I refused to go back and forth.

The great thing about being in the will of GOD is you will know instantly when the devil is trying to attack you and you can automatically start praying to let the devil know that he has no dominion over your life.

We cannot be bogged down and dragging if we want to be in a position to fight the devil off.

I'm telling you, if I have to walk through the house all day and on the job speaking to the devil, then that is what I have to do. I refuse to go down and stay down. I am challenging you to see that no matter what you have been through to not let the devil take you down.

I felt like I would never get back up after all that I had endured. I choose to accept the challenges that are being presented to me. Did it ever occur to you that the obstacles that are set up in your life may just be a test? I believe so. I think the LORD places many different tests in your life just to see how much you will bear before you decide to take off and say I'm done with this. The reward is worth it, stay in the race.

Philippians 3:14 states, "I press toward the mark for the prize of the high calling of GOD in Christ Jesus." Don't give up, don't give in. It will be greater later.

The question that always comes up is, "When will I get my breakthrough, or when will things start to look up for me?" I cannot imagine a buildup of growth in the Lord without anything coming our way. Sometimes obstacles are big and sometimes they're small.

We were all created and formed out of something that helped us to see things more clearly.

Have you ever been through something so bad that you had the nerve to question why? Well, why not? Whatever you do, do not go back to the devil's playground.

That is exactly where he wants you at. There have been plenty of times when I had to call on the Lord for comfort. I would literally be in tears because I found myself dwindling down and not coming back up.

It seemed like everything that I had been through and thought that I was coming out of was coming back to me even harder as if it just happened.

Of course, you will have moments in your life where all the same questions will come back in your head and make you think all kinds of negative thoughts. When you do have these thoughts that may be negative, turn them into positives.

If the devil says you are unworthy, turn it around and say "I am worthy." If the devil tells you that it should have been you, you can turn it around and say "No, the Lord still has plans in place for me." We need to pray when we get down and know that the Lord will pick us up.

I was told while you are in prayer and you are asking the Lord to lift you up, or pick you up, you need to speak life over yourself as well. You have the power in your tongue to speak life. You shall live. I shall live. Let us live in Jesus Mighty Name.

Psalm 119:114

Thou art my hiding place and my shield: I hope in thy word.

CHAPTER EIGHT
Hibernation

As people, we sometimes have to go into hibernation. I am not speaking of literally hiding. I am speaking of spending more time with yourself, less time on the phone, more time in your Word, and more time on the throne of GOD.

If you find yourself like me, I have to take some time-outs. As children, we learn that a time-out mainly is for punishment, but in this case, my period of shutting down in hibernation was not about punishment, but for self-growth. I had to pause, reflect, and rethink everything that was taking place in my life.

I felt myself spending too much time on the phone or in front of the television. When I found anything to be a distraction, I had to set myself apart from it, especially when I felt the Lord was trying to get my attention.

Obedience is everything when you are of service to the Lord. Sometimes you must let people know that it is not them in particular that you choose not to be open with. It is the time that you have to put away for yourself so that you can better prepare for war. This is something I had to do quite often.

Some had mistaken it for the depression that was beginning to rise up in me again, but I could not at that time share everything that the LORD had set up for me to do. One of those things was to humble myself even more and stay quiet so I could hear from Him. There is no way that you can hear from the Lord when you have so much chaos going on around you. Sometimes you can create another situation in your situation by trying to dissect it and give your input.

I have learned to not associate myself with other people's business. Once you do that, you are part of the busybody committee. The Bible speaks about being a busybody: "Did you hear," "I heard," and "What do you think of this situation?"

I will share with you that if you are going to someone else for their advice and it is not spirit led, then you may want to tread lightly.

Hibernation is a must in spiritual growth. You actually have to take some time out to pray, listen, and humble yourself through it all. There have been many times when I have had to do a complete shutdown. In the midst of it all, I have always found myself thanking and praising GOD just for peace of mind. I have never been a person consumed with the thought of being in a big audience. In this world, you have to be able to walk alone and be alone at times.

"Time out. I need to step back."

I have never heard of anyone being at a party and receiving what God has for them. Even when you go on a fast, you have to literally set yourself away from everything.

I can hear my spirit screaming out, yet it is in peace, looking for a sense of direction. Again, this is something that I could only get when I hid and sought the LORD even more. The devil has a way of playing with your mindset when you think you do not need to go into hibernation. We cannot do this walk alone. I can only see myself as a car on the freeway losing complete control of my vehicle if I did not have the correct driver.

I will say hide if you can, or not, so that you can get what the Lord is trying to get across to you.

Have you ever laid under the covers, and found yourself peeking out from under them? Well, that was (and is) me at times. My grandmother Pauline McNair used to say, "Stop looking in the oven, it ain't done yet." This is how I feel.

I am not done yet, and there are plenty more times when I will have to be placed back in the oven until I am ready to move on to the next level that the Lord has for me.

So, I will say that it is okay to turn off your phone and turn down some outings. It is all worth it. The Lord will wait until He gets you to Himself to speak to your heart. It's all worth it.

James 1:22

But be ye doers of the word, and not hearers only, deceiving your own selves.

REFLECTIONS

CHAPTER NINE
Self-Deception

After I had accepted my calling and spent time with the Lord and the words that He spoke to my heart, I began to fall back into depression. Yes, I said depression.

After all, the Lord had shown me, I still was going in and out. I discovered during this process what I was going through. I knew at that moment I was deceiving myself. I was running from what was truly designed for my life.

I remember when I was just a young girl (around 11 years old) and going to the church that my grandmother attended. I truly enjoyed going to church, even

Sunday school. However, I was quick to respond to someone when asked if I liked attending church, saying, "No, I do not," thinking that this was what they wanted to hear. All along, my grandmother Pauline McNair had seen something in me at a young age.

The words she spoke to me were, "It won't be hard for you to live a Christian-based life."

I responded and said, "What do you mean?" She said, "I just know." It is now 28 years later, and I was still struggling with receiving what was already designed for me, and that was to teach the word, and not preach.

I truly believe that just because you are a teacher does not mean you are a preacher. I am not there yet, but I am going to let the Lord use me as He sees fit.

Have you ever been through something and during the course of it, you absolutely knew what was for you, but you still were going back and forth about it? This might just be what God has for you.

Don't doubt what you know is true. There is a song that says, "What GOD has for me, it is for me." This is so true. We all have a specific assignment in our lives; some of us may have more than one. The song also goes on to say, "I know without a doubt, He's going to bring me out."

"Mirror, Mirror"

I never thought that I would come out of many things, but I did, and I am not saying that I am completely out. However, I will say I am coming out, moving on, and living in it all at once.

I woke up one morning, shortly after I realized that I was deceiving myself about many things in my life. I tried to make myself think that all was okay and that I was and could be comfortable in the state I was in, but clearly, I was not.

My pastor once told a story about a frog and that particular reptile was warming up to a temperature of comfort. I said to myself, "I am this frog." I can no longer be comfortable with being in a state of comfort when in reality, it is truly a mess.

Have you ever seen or been in a mess and tried to make the best of it? It happens. Did you ever decide that yes, although this is a situation of chaos, you would still try to make the best out of it and reason with it, choosing to make all the excuses in the world?

That is what I was dealing with. However, this time around, I no longer wanted to be the frog who was comfortable sitting in the same boat with the same water, making myself think that everything was okay. The worst deception is self-deception. It is one thing when someone is trying to deceive you, but it is another thing when you are deceiving yourself.

Do not be that frog who lays low and thinks that things will change by sitting in the same environment.

There is a saying that states, "When reality sets in, you see things from a different perspective." Do not allow your reality to be buried for too long. Rise up with me and step out of the boat. The sooner you can identify "the greater you," the sooner you will no longer allow yourself to be set back. I had been thinking to myself about how I had allowed the tricks of the devil to deter my walk, my journey, and my overall growth; but not anymore. I speak to deception right now in Jesus' mighty name, that it no longer has a place in my life. You can also speak greatness into your life.

I have decided that it was time to evict the devil and keep him out. I will no longer allow the devil to take up space in my mind, my heart, or my growth. He has officially been served a notice and he must leave immediately.

There was no more room for the chaos that I was dealing with. We all know that the mind is a battlefield. Help me say it, "Devil you have to flee." I will tell you what I had to tell myself: pick up your left foot and stomp on his head.

Now pick up your right foot and do the same. When we are children of GOD, we have the authority to do just that.

1 John 5:4

For whatsoever is born of God overcometh the world: and this is the victory that overcometh the world, even our faith.

CHAPTER TEN
Victory Is Mine

I am proclaiming in my everyday walk that the Lord will continually fight all my battles, mentally, physically, and emotionally.

There is a song that we often sing, an old hymn that says, "Victory is mine." No matter what it looks like, this world can throw whatever at me, and I know that the Lord will have my front, my back, and my side.

The scripture of Deuteronomy 20:4 states this, "For the Lord, your GOD is he that goeth with you, to fight for you, against your enemies to save you." The greatest battle is that of the mind. Once the devil gets in your mind, he can sway you in almost any direction if you are not prayed up.

One time in church, the pastor stated that no matter what you are going through, your desire to please the Lord has to be greater than your pleasures of the world.

He also said if you are not living your life according to the lifestyle that was created for you, then it will be easy for the devil to play on your mindset.

The devil does not bother you when you are doing his work. So of course, during my Christian transition, I was faced with many things because I refused to fall into the enemy's traps.

People probably assumed that I was crazy. I would be walking through the stores, even at work speaking and telling the devil that he had no dominion over me. After I would declare what needed to be said, the devil would flee, but of course he will show himself again in any angle.

"I am winning. You are winning. We won!"

On one occasion, I had attempted something very major (yes, it was major to me). My husband is a dance instructor, and he teaches children how to Mime dance. I had gone into one of his classes and sat in the back of the church with the courage I had built up to go inside.

As I saw the children dancing, the devil immediately began to play on my mind.

I did not see my daughter up there dancing and I became angry and bitter all over again. I walked out immediately, hoping that he did not or could not see the pain on my face.

I got into my car and started crying hysterically (yes, in rage, anger, and every emotion that you could think of). I started the car, hooked up my device, and turned on my Pandora.

The song that came on was "He Turned It" by Tye Tribbett. I began to listen to the words of that song. He will turn it all around for you. The song states, "The devil thought he had me."

I had to speak to myself and say "Melissa, you have the victory." Even when my days are long and the clouds seem to hang low, I know the Lord has me. He is an unchanging GOD, and he will never fail me. The enemy knows how to pierce your heart and soul. He knew that prior to my heart being healed, I would see children my daughter's age and how it would affect me. He also knew that I wanted to support my husband in his dance practices and that it was a difficult task for me to sit through them.

*Later that day, I went home to read my Bible, and I was led to go through my daughter's things. I had not been through her papers in quite some time because I thought it would reactivate my pain. I picked up her Bible and as I started to turn the pages, I saw the letters that she had written to **GOD**.*

I started to cry. I mean the tears poured down, but this time, they were tears of joy. I said, "Yes, Lord."

I continued to read. She knew exactly where her help came from. If my 12-year-old daughter knew who to run to, then I definitely needed to remember where my help came from.

I could not ask for anything more. She had a relationship with God. That meant a lot to me. She was the kind of kid who did not say much but observed everything.

A few months down the line, my mother had become ill. One of my main wishes was for my mother to develop a relationship with Christ. During her illness, she never questioned GOD, nor did she lack in her faith. She was committed. She did everything she could do as a servant (unless she had a restriction), and even with her limitations, she still was working for the LORD.

She gave GOD all the glory and honor that He deserved. She would stand up and give her testimony at any given moment. She did not care who was in service or who saw or heard her. She wanted the Saints to know what He was doing for her.

I had a conversation with my mother one evening out of the many times we had talked. She said "Melissa, let me ask you a question." I said, "Yes Mom, what is it?" She said, "How do people not believe that there is a GOD? How do they think that the birds and the animals of the world got here?

How do the organs that we have in our body get inside of us?" I said, "Mom, I have no idea. None of this was made by man, and they need to know it." It then dawned on me that my mom was in it to win it, yes, the prize.

Victory is mine. We are all in this Christian race and we all will be granted the desires of our hearts if we just hang in there. One of my mother's favorite songs was,

"Faithful is Our GOD." He is faithful to the last drop of our time here.

He granted me and my family the time to spend with my mother, and even on her sickbed, he gave grace and mercy to us. He granted us time, even to the point where I feel that my mother had made peace with the Lord, and it was up to us on this side of the Earth to accept that she had received her invitation into heaven.

So, I will say it again, I got the victory!! I was sitting alongside her bed reading in the book of Thessalonians and I saw out of my peripheral vision, a small, shaped spirit beam. I was so shaken.

I just kept reading, even though I knew what I saw was actually there. My head would not turn to get a complete look; however, I felt a warm feeling go all over my body.

My mother laid there still looking up as if she had been viewing something so beautiful that she could not take her eyes off it. At that moment, I knew what was going on. Still, in awe, I just kept reading to her. Shortly after I had been sitting there for a while, the respiratory therapist came in and said to me, "I did not know that you had your child with you.

We are technically not allowed to have children on the floor due to the Covid policies, but we can make an exception this time."

I could not even speak. I was in disbelief. He saw what I had seen. He then went on to say, "Where did your little one go?"

My response was, "I did not bring

anyone with me." I will still say to this day that I don't know exactly who it was, but it was shaped and glowing like an angel.

My mother had already received her invitation from the Lord. How could I not rejoice in the time that He had granted? I've got many reasons to keep praising the LORD.

BONDAGE BREAKTHROUGH BLESSINGS

Reflection

John 8:32

And ye shall know the truth, and the truth shall make you free.

CHAPTER ELEVEN
Breakthrough

The chains are beginning to fall. Even though I had the victory, and I was coming out of the depression, I still had some chains that needed to be released from me. There were some wounds that were reopened.

My mother is my queen always and losing her just made me revert to some of the bad feelings that I used to carry around; this included sorrow, sadness, and emptiness. It seemed like everything that I had been set free from had come back ten times stronger.

The first lady of my church had a talk with me, and her words were *very valuable. I never take her words for granted. She saw me slipping. It is such a blessing to have someone care enough about you that they pay attention and notice that you are not yourself. I truly thank GOD for that alone.*

I was very aware that I had been carrying extra weight on me and I am not speaking of body weight. I am speaking of negative things in life that hold you down. When we go through life, it is so imperative to have people around us that can build us up and walk the same Christian walk that we do.

A true sister or brother in Christ will see the barriers and pray for you around the clock. Unfortunately, we will have all kinds of darts through it all, but we must be willing to get through it.

I was going through this even more during the time of my mother's passing. I had fallen right back in the same trap of feeling down, depressed, and lost. Sometimes, even as Christians, we still need someone to pick us up so that we can break out of what has us bound. I was walking around, yet again, full of hurt and pain from losing my best friend.

"I feel it. The break."

My mother was everything to me. I was on a good path after her passing, but there were many days I would just get in my vehicle and ride around hoping that my phone would ring so that I could hear her say, "Hey, what you doing? I need to go get some things done." I was always up and ready to be of service to my mother and was proud to do anything she needed me to do.

I had claimed the victory, yet at the same time, allowed the devil to make his way back into my world. Something needed to be done. I recognized that I had made another trip to Misery Lane and needed to get back on Hope Street.

The first step in any rehabilitation is realizing that there is a problem, the second step is identifying exactly what those issues are, and the last step is dealing with it and coming up with a solution. The main thought that kept coming to my head was, "Do I want to stay in this, or do I want to come out?"

I had already been in this place before and it was so evident that it was holding me back in my spiritual growth.

I knew my calling. I accepted my calling. I have many times claimed my victory over and over, knowing there was no going back to the dark places that the devil likes to see people in. I began reading my Word more, praying more, and fasting so that I could hear from the LORD.

The truth is that when you have so much going on around you and are not allowing enough time for GOD, you miss out on a lot.

I will tell anyone that anytime you feel depression coming, get ready to go into a spiritual war. When you have so much to offer and the LORD is working with you, you can rest assured that the devil is somewhere plotting to see what he can do to you next.

There have been times when the Lord has spoken to me in my dreams. I had a dream during this period of my life. I was definitely at a standstill in my spiritual life and even though I had not given my full service to the LORD, He still was not done with me. I laid down one evening. I can clearly remember the date.

It was May 18, 2020. I will never forget this night. When I was sleeping, there appeared to be a chair that sat up high. It was not very clear, but it was enough for me to see that it was a chair with two arms, and in the chair appeared to be a man whose image was of how one would describe the LORD.

He spoke these words to me. He said "I am the WAY, the LIGHT, and the TRUTH.

In my sleep, I felt my heart stop beating. I sat straight up in the bed and gasped for my breath. I was so overwhelmed by what had just occurred. The Lord was telling me that I could in no way make it to Him unless I had, yet again, cleansed my heart.

Your heart is connected with everything else. If your heart is not pure, there is no way to make it in the beautiful gates of heaven. I am so thankful once again.

I do know and can tell you from experience that if you are bitter and angry, you cannot, and will not be able to grow in the Lord.

The bitterness I was carrying was normal for when you lose someone, but when you are trying to move forward in your walk, it can hinder anyone. I know that my mother would not have wanted me to be angry, bitter, or saddened because she gained her reward in heaven. It is up to me to make it there as well.

There are many reasons why people are stuck and are not able to move ahead. It is not worth it. A broken heart can take you out of this world with your work undone. Let your works for the Lord be fulfilled.

If you are incarcerated in your own pain, it's time to break free. Step out, break free from the chains, and walk away. I mean it. Walk away, even if it looks like you cannot move. There is always a way to escape.

2 Corinthians 5:17

Therefore if any man be in Christ, he is a new creature: old things are passed away; behold, all things are become new.

CHAPTER *TWELVE*
Moving On

We all come to a place in our lives where we have to move on and leave the past in the past. Sometimes we cannot move ahead because we are stuck in our past life. Yes, we all want to move ahead, but for whatever reason, we become stagnant in the process of growth.

We can think of many things that can and will hold us back, such as death, love, and relationships, but as for me, I want to move on. I heard someone say, "You can move as fast as you want, but you cannot move at all without a plan."

My plan was to serve the Lord, f

follows His Word, and be the greatest servant ever, but some things had to go before I could call myself a true servant of GOD.

I had so much junk that needed to be thrown out that it was ridiculous, and I am not speaking of only material things. People and things were in the way of my growth. Have you ever seen a flower grow that was not getting its proper water and treatment? No, you have not. Eventually, it will die off. There is nothing that grows without the proper nurturing.

Dead ends in your hair are another example of nurturing. I can relate. Many things grow that are being cut off. Hair alone cannot grow when it is not given the proper care. As people, if you do not have individuals in your life that can bring the best out of you, then you have to by all means cut them out of your life. If you think about the circle you have, how many of them are for you? How many are against you?

It may sound a little upsetting to do some deep digging but moving ahead calls for a checklist and examination of what is helping you, as well as what and who is hurting you. My pastor once spoke about people who are not of the same lifestyle, as you may need a closer look, but most of all start with yourself.

I started my growth journey by looking into myself, first, to see what all needed to be done. I found many things that needed attention, and once I was able to identify those not-so-great things about myself, I was then able to move ahead to focus on what was around me. Everything starts from within yourself. When I think about the process of cleaning, I think about where it all begins. Is your heart pure? Do you walk what you talk? Are you about your father's business?

I went through the list checking things off. I got to the last question and said, "Well, I could be doing way more that is for sure." Once I came to grips with that, I understood even more that if I was doing more of the Lord's work and less of what I wanted to do, then I would be in better shape, mentally, physically, and emotionally.

The mental part of me needed to be fed more, but I couldn't be fed more if I was allowing time for everything else but the Word, GOD, and His teachings. I cannot be physically okay if I find that I put more time and energy into chasing anything other than what the Lord is providing. Spiritually, we must learn to take care of our temple. So, anything that the Lord does not approve of has to be removed.

Your emotional state can become very rigid if you do not grow some skin. I am not talking about the skin on your body. I am referring to going through an emotional state and being able to accept what is being said or done. If not, you won't be able to move ahead in anything.

Have you ever seen a rug that will not lay flat? Can you picture that very rug with all the things under it that you've been covering up, scared to let go of, or just not ready to deal with it yet? I don't know about you, but it was time to pull the rug up, sweep out the mess, and be done.

"New address"

There is generally one day out of the

week when you take out your trash and put it on the street. Let us take out the trash and leave it there, even at the recycling bins. Just know that everything is not meant to be recycled in your life. Let us all move on and move to pass anything that is not growing and nurturing the greatness in you.

I believe that there is such greatness in each one of us, it just has to be activated. GOD designed us all to be conquerors and achieve great things in our lives. He did not intend for us to be on the bottom, but on top. I know He wants the best for me. He wants the best for you as well.

The GOD we serve wants to see us rise up and not fall. He provided us with all the weapons we need to get through life. Sometimes, we cannot see the best in ourselves and others around us may not tell you how wonderful you are. However, once you move past what is and what can hinder you, then you will be blessed in so many ways.

You just have to move on and not look back. Recently, I just started listening to singer Johnathan McReynolds and his song, "Moving On." One of the lyrics says, "I know my rearview can't compare to what God will do with my life ..."

Do I believe that? Yes, I do with my whole heart. He has big plans for all of us. Many times, when we walk, we have a tendency to look back and see all the ground that we have covered, and goals that we have accomplished. Let us look forward and focus on the many blessings that are in store.

1 Peter 2:9

But ye are a chosen generation, a royal priesthood, an holy nation, a peculiar people; that ye should shew forth the praises of him who hath called you out of darkness into his marvelous light.

CHAPTER THIRTEEN

Different Faces

I have to put on many different faces to get through the days, and I still keep praising GOD through it all. I can absolutely say the baggage of everything that I have carried has now been released. We as people, and this can be for everyone, can be carrying the weight of the world on our shoulders and no one would ever know, especially if you do not speak about it.

There are so many of us in this world that are walking around with pain built up and are wearing many masks to hide it. Which mask do you have on now? How many times can you continue to change your mask before anyone even notices?

Pain is one emotion that will grow and eventually, will show on one's appearance. Anyone can laugh and act as if everything is okay. The downside to this is that you will not get better, the recovery process becomes longer, and you will never heal.

What does it mean to heal? The healing process does not happen overnight. If you accept that there is an issue and you are ready to deal with it, then that is the first step. I didn't want to admit that I needed help. I was suffering mentally. I just wanted to be alone, lights low, and didn't want anyone around; this seemed to be the remedy for me. I know this is definitely a sign of depression. There is a saying that goes along the lines of "You can run, but you can't hide." I was literally running from myself, believing that it was normal to not come out of the darkness. I thought that as long as I had a different mask to put on for the day, then it all would work out for me. We all know that many people wear several masks and carry on many different characters to cover up their pain. They do it so that people think that everything is normal.

The question I had to ask myself was, "Is it possible to go through your whole life being someone else because of the pain that is buried within, simply because you do not want to deal with the situation at hand?" I did not want to be one of those people. I looked in the mirror one day and did not like what I was seeing.

"Who am I today?"

The devil was having his way with

me. I saw a mess. Yes, a mess. I cried and I said no more will I allow Satan to control my life whenever he feels like stepping in. I had to speak some authority over myself while looking in the mirror. I know that it may sound crazy, but it is true.

I feel it is absolutely necessary to do some self-evaluation over your own life, some inspection. I had come to the conclusion that a lot of the pain that I was carrying (that led me to wear different masks) was caused by me. I needed to be delivered from myself. Yes, it is true.

Sometimes we have to walk away from ourselves and back into the will of God. I was of His will, but not in his will. He knows my name so well, and he is my Comforter in all things. So, why did I have to go through so much to realize that?

This is where the inspection part comes in. I didn't even have to be anyone else in the Lord. He knew me for who I was and the same goes for you. We don't have to put on many masks and act out many characters to make it through difficult days. He is our everything, so there is no need to add extra layers of extra pain to ourselves when we can be just who He designed us to be. He already knew what would take place in our lives and the path that we all have to go down.

I know for a fact that He will not put anything on us that we cannot bear. He does not work like that, but I do feel that the Lord will test you with many trials just to see how long you will hang in there, or how much you will trust him.

I found myself being guilty of doubting GOD and actually, at times, feeling like I would go through my whole life looking for a mask to put on every day. This was no option for me either. I could not in any way have the mindset of doubting Thomas. I know what the Lord can do. I have seen many miracles and I have even witnessed His work myself.

If you are like me and you have to put on many masks to cope, please know (whether or not we have on the mask) that GOD knows our pain. Be healed, be delivered, and be set free. I would hear my pastor say this quite often, however, to receive what the Lord has for you, you have to come to Him bare with no covering. Anything that is covered does not heal properly. Remove the mask and start your healing process. He is waiting for you to open the door.

Reflections

Joshua 22:5

But take diligent heed to do the commandment and the law, which Moses the servant of the LORD charged you, to love the LORD your God, and to walk in all his ways, and to keep his commandments, and to cleave unto him, and to serve him with all your heart and with all your soul.

CHAPTER *FOURTEEN*

It's Not About You Or Me

How many times through our trials and tribulations do we forget that it is not about us? We have to understand that whatever tribulations we go through in this life, they're not always about us or because we did something wrong.

The truth is if something happens, whether it is big or small, nothing can happen without the Lord's permission. When we are faced with tragedy or change, it is not always for us but for the next person. I know this may sound insane to a person. In the body of Christ, if your brother is suffering, then we should be able to pick them up.

It is not for us to look down on them or speak negatively about them, but to help carry their weight and deal with it the way the Lord would see fit. In the scripture Galatians 6:2, it states, "Bear ye one another burdens, and so fulfill the law of Christ." This is what the best book says, the Word of GOD.

One of our main tasks on this earth is to fulfill the laws of Christ. I know some people feel that other people's business is not their concern if the person chooses not to tell their whole life story (or the bare minimum).

If someone says to pray for them and you consider yourself a Christian, by all means you should pray. We do not have to know everything that is going on in a person's life to go before GOD on their behalf. There are, in some cases, people who feel that if it does not concern them, then it is not their problem. Well, again, if you are in the body of Christ, technically, it's not your duty to solve anything. However, it is our reasonable service to pray.

I know as I go through and have been going through, there have been a lot of people who were praying and have prayed for me. Every prayer meant so much to me. When we can pray each other through the storms of life, we then can tell our testimonies.

Testimonies are very important. I will share a testimony with you that happened to me back in 2005. I was working at the Embassy hotel in housekeeping and around this time I was having seizures. For some unknown reason, the neurologist could not tell me why I was having them.

"Remove self. It is necessary."

I was in a room cleaning, and we had a lead inspector and a boss who would come by the rooms to check to see if the rooms were considered completed and ready for check-in. This particular leader that I had would really be on me at times and I did not really know why. I waited for two days after the incident to return to work.

Prior to me cleaning this room, I had some seizure activity and was taken out by the ambulance from work. However, I was determined to return to work. I had to clean a room this Saturday morning and I will never forget it.

My eyes were running so I wore sunglasses to work and was never questioned about why I came to work like that, but my manager did witness my eyes running side to side.

I carried on with my day and had cleaned my first room. It took way longer than expected. Can you imagine your eye running while trying to clean up? I told myself I am not going home, and that I could do this. I was not going to base my day off of how I felt, but what all that I could accomplish while feeling this way.

I went on to the next room which was a mess. I started in the bathroom and worked my way out to the bedroom. This room had twin beds that had a nightstand that sat in between them with a lamp. I had stripped the beds, applied new sheets, wiped down the surfaces, and vacuumed.

I had become very overwhelmed with

my eyes and with not having a clear focus. I sat down on the bed and started praying, "Lord, help me. Lord, I need you right now." I had prayed previously before, but this prayer was sincere, genuine, and truly from the heart. I found out on this day that He is our everything and the only one that can change all situations.

I sat there for a few more minutes and prayed even harder. I turned on Praise 1490 and started listening to the music, and not just the beat. I let the music minister to my heart. As I continued praying, tears ran down my face and I felt like my eyes were ripping, as if something was tearing my eyes into pieces. This feeling lasted for a few minutes.

I got up off the bed and finished cleaning the room. I was running behind at this point, but me taking the time out to pray to the Lord helped me to gain some strength and continue to clean my rooms.

I made sure that I did a good job vacuuming and walked through the room once again to be sure that everything was in place. I went on to my next room and started working.

About 10 minutes into cleaning the room, I heard my lead say to me, "Can you come back to the room you just did? There is something I need to show you." I said, "Okay that is fine." I stopped working in the room I was in and walked back into the other room.

She said "Look down there. What is that on the ground? It looks like little pieces of glass." I picked them up. It was like pieces of what appeared to be glass that, I was feeling being torn from my eyes. I smiled and she said, "What is funny?

I should not have to come back and find little things like this on the floor. What in the heck is that anyways? I have never seen anything like that?"

I said that is the evidence of my healing. She said, "What do you mean?" I took off my shades. My eyes were very irritated, but no longer running. She looked me in the eyes, said "Oh, my Lord," and walked away. She didn't bother me anymore that day.

I had experienced healing and it needed to be known. It was not only for me, but also for someone else's healing.

Two weeks later, she asked me to start sending her scriptures and she eventually started going to church. I will honestly say at that point in my life, I was far from being where I needed to be.

*I was taken on a journey and through this particular journey, my life had been transformed. Don't hold back on what **GOD** has done for you but be a testimony for someone else to be healed. Let us keep in mind that it is not about us, but about **GOD** and His will for us.*

Proverbs 3:5-6

Trust in the LORD with all thine heart; And lean not unto thine own understanding. In all thy ways acknowledge him, and he shall direct thy paths.

CHAPTER *SEVENTEEN*

Better Days Are Coming

How many days have you woke up with the intention of having a blessed and fulfilling day, but something so small messes up your whole morning?

I have had so many days like this. It got to the point where I had to make notes to guide me into what I had expected for myself. The excuses that I would come up with were ridiculous.

There are many times we can say that the devil is busy, but the truth is we actually allow it. I came to a decision that the devil would not be able to dictate my days anymore.

If the Lord allowed me to see another day, then I needed to make the best of it. We all know that the next day, hour, or second is not promised to anyone, and none of us knows our check-out date.

I am sharing this with you and maybe it will work for you. When you wake up in the morning, write down 3-4 things that you are happy about and focus on those things.

If you can only think of 2 things or maybe even 1, then that is good enough because the first blessing is waking up in the morning and knowing that the Lord has given you another day on this side of the earth.

I don't know about you, but I have spent too much time putting off what could have been done last week or the week before.

I decided to challenge myself, invest in myself, and give more back to myself. I want the Lord to know that what he has invested in me was worth it. I was meant to be here and the gifts that he planted in me need to be unwrapped and rolled out. I don't want to waste any more time compromising with myself and blaming the devil in between.

I got up on a Saturday morning and went to the bathroom and when I looked in the mirror, I did not like what I saw. So, I had a conversation with myself and said these words, "When are you going to get off the devil's clock?

I want to have better days, and I will." You have to speak over yourself, encourage yourself, and know that better days are coming, only if you allow them to. We have more control over our lives and our days than we think. We just have to allow GOD to stay in the center of our lives.

"Yesterday was yesterday. Leave it there."

The very moment that you can walk alone, you will see just how far you can get. I don't even know how I got this far in life. I accepted Christ into my life in late 2017 and was still not in a good place for years.

I can honestly say that before the Lord saved my soul and I proclaimed my calling and walk, it seemed as if I had a lot of good days. However, as we all know, the devil does not bother you when you are on his turf and are doing exactly what he wants you to do.

How many times did you think

you were doing something, but later on found out that you were doing nothing but wasting your own time? I am so glad that I am in the Lord now.

The feeling of being wrapped in the LORD's love is the best thing. The best part of my life now is that when I do have bad days, I do not have to turn to the world, which only made me worse. I can turn to my Word and know that the Lord will pull me out.

Let all your days be intentionally great. If you find yourself slipping and if you think you are about to have a bad day, then reflect back on what you are grateful for. There is no such thing as a good day every day, but every day should be a great day when you have breath in your body.

Make a decision today that you will

have a good day every day, even when it looks bad. Our days can be so much worse... but GOD.

Have you ever sat back and thought about another person's situation and said to yourself, "You have no reason to be upset about anything at all?" I remember when my mother was going through her chemo treatments. She was having a really bad day.

We had approached the building where she would be getting her treatment and she said, "I am so sick of coming here, even though I have not gotten sick as what people had expected from these treatments, I am just tired."

My mother went through many rounds of treatment and when she would go to the hospital, she would stay anywhere from 5-9 days depending on her blood counts. We got up to the second floor to head to see her oncologist. She would always see her physician for her orders and would head upstairs to the third floor for her stay. We used to call it her monthly mini-vacation to make some light of her being there.

We sat in the living room area, and along came a woman who was very weak being accompanied by her family. She was pushing her pole through and could barely stand up. At this moment, my mother looked over at me and said, "Never mind what I had spoken." I said, "Oh yeah mom, it could be worse."

My mother had a lot of bad days, but from that day on she had decided that no matter what she was faced with, that she would make the best out of it.

I could in no way understand what she was feeling, but whenever she was feeling sad, I also felt sad. She was my mother, and despite what she felt, I did not always let my true pain show. Decide today just what type of days you want to have from this point on.

There will be bad days, and I am a witness to the dark days. However, as soon as you recognize the cloud that is trying to hang over your head, then reverse it and make it better.

We have the power to change our environment and our circumstances. They say to watch what you speak. In this case, speak greatness and watch how your life will change for the better.

There will be times when we fall. There may even be times where we may lose sight of what is right in front of us, but just do not fall out of line. I believe that as long as you keep pushing through, the Lord will not leave you to fall out and stay out. There is always better to come when you are ready to receive it.

Psalm 55:2

Attend unto me, and hear me: I mourn in my complaint, and make a noise.

CHAPTER SIXTEEN
Faith Avenue

Where is your faith? Is your faith the kind that you pray about and let go of? Or do you pray to God and believe that it is coming to pass? I do understand that we all have situations where we want to believe that God can, and he will fix your issues.

However, when He is not moving as fast as you want Him to, you start doubting Him. I had this issue really badly. I knew many things, especially what the LORD can and will do. He has even shown me on many occasions.

Yet, I was still putting my prayer requests into the Lord and then interfering in GOD'S business. I had so many setbacks while trying to grow in the Lord because of the fact that I was the setback. I admit I was the problem.

We have to stop treating our GOD like a man. He doesn't need any third party when you come to Him. If I had been obedient a long time ago and let Him work, then I would have made it further than where I am now.

There is a scripture in Matthew 7:7-8 that states, "Ask, and it shall be given to you: seek and ye shall find; knock and it shall be opened unto you, for everyone that asketh receiveth: and he that seeketh findeth: and to him that knocketh; it shall be open."

Listen very carefully. He did not say ask and doubt. He did not say ask, walk away, and give up because the door did not open up right away. We must learn to follow instructions and have faith.

I want to reflect on a few things. After I decided to get back into the work field, nothing seemed to work out for me. Every job I thought I wanted I did not get, and everything that I was praying for did not come to pass. I started to feel like the Lord was intentionally ignoring me because my faith was wearing down, and my faith was wearing down due to my lack of being in my Word.

You have to make sure that you have the proper tools in this world. We have to believe and know that the Lord only wants the best for us. Have you ever had someone come to you for advice, but they say, "I need you to keep this between me and you?"

A few weeks pass on and the very thing they told you, they told someone else. I know this has happened to many people, but this is where we have completely taken GOD out of the equation. All we need is Him.

I had to learn this the hard way. I had voided out so many answers and prayer requests from the Lord because I had involved someone else and their opinion. Guess what? I have already lost the battle. The God that we serve is big enough to handle every request that is presented to Him, but we have to keep the faith.

I think that sometimes our faith fails when we do not get that desire that we want. It is completely okay to have a prayer partner or someone that you can confide in but do understand where our blessings come from. Sometimes there are some prayers that are never answered, and your faith may be tested even more. Can I share this with you? Think of a situation when GOD did not respond at all, and time is still passing by. It is not always going to be a YES.

There are many things that the Lord will see and say, "not right now" or just plain "NO." He knows what is best. I believe that the Lord will block some things in your life if He feels that you are not ready to deal with it. He may feel that He doesn't want you in that environment, or just simply may have something way better in store for you, so no matter what it looks like, don't throw in the towel. It is not over.

Have you ever been rejected by someone or something and you just really thought that it was the last resort? I think we all had that experience in some form, and it eventually passes over. I'm sure when you looked back you were able to say to yourself, "Oh, that's why." GOD works in mysterious ways.

The things that you think would break you are what can make you. Getting others involved who are not on the same walk as you can cause you destruction. What GOD has for you is for you. Believe that with everything in you. It is not "what you want for you is for you."

Years could pass and you still do not hear anything back from GOD. Just keep in mind that He steers the wheel of our lives, and we want to allow him to be the captain of our ship at all times.

I want to just give an example of how things can look from a worldly view. We all have at least one person that we can talk to in the natural, meanwhile, we have also spoken our requests to the Lord. We all are human, so we tend to get discouraged from time to time, which is absolutely natural.

"Where are you at spiritually?"

I find that because we are not getting a response back as fast as we want to, we go seeking other opinions. If we want GOD to guide us and lead us in the right directions in life, let us keep the faith and remain humble. Let us not be so quick to move about when we do not hear anything. The best and most accurate answers come from our Lord and Savior. He created and designed us with a purpose.

Keep this scripture close to you. "Now Faith is the Substance of things hoped for, the evidence of things not seen." Now is the *keyword, not later, not tomorrow, but now! Is your faith activated or barely working? James 2:26 states, "For as the body without the spirit is dead, so faith without works is dead also." Wake up the faith that is buried in you and watch **GOD** work.*

Jeremiah 17:7-8

Blessed is the man that trusteth in the LORD, and whose hope the LORD is. For he shall be as a tree planted by the waters, and that spreadeth out her roots by the river, and shall not see when heat cometh, but her leaf shall be green; and shall not be careful in the year of drought, neither shall cease from yielding fruit

CHAPTER *EIGHTEEN*

Trust Fall

Do you trust GOD during all of your difficult times in life? Do you see yourself leaning on your own understanding? I can tell you from my experience that when we do this, we put ourselves at risk for falling. Consider yourself standing and falling back with no cushion. That very fall may take you out depending on the situation.

My youngest daughter will get in front of me, and she will say, "Mom catch me," and I will say, "Why do you like doing this?" She said, "It makes me feel good when I know that you are there to catch me." I thought to myself that yes this is good, but there is something that is greater than me, and that is GOD. He is the Author, and the Perfecter of our faith.

I explained to her in that moment that, yes, I am your mother and I will always be here to pick you up, but even when I can pick you up, you should always depend on GOD. He can not only pick you up, but He can also keep you during the trials and tribulations that you will face.

Children also need to know who to trust when they fall. I have fallen many times during my journey to recovery and there was only one who could pick me up, minister to my soul, and keep me when I was down and out.

I am not saying that I did not trust other people. I absolutely had a few people who I could turn to during my storm. Even in the words that they spoke, at the end of all conversations and therapy it would be the phrase, "Lean on the Lord," and that is all I've been doing and will keep doing.

Have you ever fallen to the ground and looked up, and as you were looking up, you also looked around to see who was all looking?

Even if someone was looking or could assist you, they still could not ease your pain or fix your injury. There are times when we do fall and sometimes it's because the Lord will sit us down for his glory.

"Uh oh Lord, I'm falling!

I remember one time a few years back, I was busy running around and worked every shift I could because I had become the person who just could not get enough of shopping. I had forgotten all about church and being before God. One particular day, He decided to get my attention, and when he did, I had no choice but to fall on Him and focus on His Word and desires for me.

My priorities were all over the place. I had everyone to fall on when I was in a good position, but when it all fell apart, I could do nothing but lay there and look up. Once you get on your back, you automatically start to examine yourself, and what it is that you may have done wrong. There are also times when the Lord just slows you down because He sees that you are overexerting yourself.

When we say we trust in the Lord, let it be consistent. He is reliable and He is the true vine. We can battle with and be uncertain about many things, but one thing that stands is the Word of GOD. Have you ever put on a pair of skates (if you are someone like myself who does not know how to skate), and your balance was off?

This is a time when you just automatically call out the Lord's name and say, "Oh! Lord, please don't let me fall." The same thing happens when we are going through life. We can speak it in our daily lives. He knows everything about us.

1 Peter 5:7 states, "Casting all your cares upon him for he careth for you." He certainly does! How many times have you gone to someone and poured your whole heart out, and after you did that, you felt in your heart that they really could care less about anything you said? It happens. Not everyone is like this, but with GOD you already know that He heard you, He cares, and He will work it out for you.

You do not have to second guess or wonder if what you just shared reached the homes of others. I do believe that GOD does place certain people in your life who will guide you, be there when you fall, pray with you, and love on you when you need it.

I do not think that the Lord would want you to keep everything bottled up and not go to your brothers or sisters in Christ. Just make sure when you do, that the person is someone that GOD placed in your life to minister to you when you feel broken, or want to give up, or are placed in a situation where you can only look up.

The reason why you want to have strong people around you that walk with Christ and live a Christian lifestyle is that, when you feel yourself on the brink of a breakdown, you could reach out to that particular person or people. The remedy to staying in and not drifting away is being so occupied with the Lord's work that you do not have time to entertain the devil.

There are so many things besides reading your Bible that you can do. If you become active in your church or pick up more duties, then that is less time for the devil to steer you the wrong way. Most of us can pray for ourselves not to fall.

We know ourselves better than anyone and even when we do not want to share anything with anyone, just know that the Lord hears all of our cries inside and out. When you do fall, fall on the LORD. He will catch you, lift you back up, and renew your strength.

REFLECTIONS

Matthew 11:28

Come unto me, all ye that labour and are heavy laden, and I will give you rest.

CHAPTER NINETEEN

Staying Grounded

There are times when we have come out of the storm and, as we are coming out, there seems to be a hiccup here and there that tries to get your attention. There is not a day that goes by that I do not think about everything that I have been through.

I have to admit, there are times when I do start to get real down and feeling like everything is closing in on me again. Have you ever felt like the devil was sitting on your shoulder reminding you of your pain and the baggage that you still have?

I'm talking about that sack that you carry around every day, but only you *can see it, and only you know it is there, because you handle it so well. I know I have. Sometimes it feels like the devil is sitting on my shoulder reminding me of the dark days that I have experienced.*

I will say that when this happens, one thing I do is I get in my Word and start praying. The more Word that is in you and the deeper you are in the Lord, the more the devil will fight you.

However, you just keep fighting on. I will generally go to my Bible with no specific scripture in mind. I say to the Lord, "Take me to where you want me to be Lord." I am one who believes that the Lord will lead and instruct you about the specific location you need to be at in the Word of God.

There is always a reason for why

He does what He does. I made up in my mind that I will not entertain the devil. People can be their worst enemies. This is where we both have to take accountability for our actions. Sometimes, we need to look in the mirror and get rid of ourselves. If reading your Word is not enough, get on your knees and pray until you fall asleep, if that is what it takes.

"Let the soil settle."

It is so obvious the devil wants us to stay in his camp, but as I had spoken about being incarcerated earlier in this book, don't make your way out and sign back in under any circumstances if you can help it. Each one of us should do a little inventory of our lives to see exactly what needs to be adjusted as we are going through our lives.

Do you see a plant that needs to

be watered and the first thing that you think is to throw it away? We don't have to be so quick to throw away or give up when things get bad. The plant just may need some water. If you see that your lamp is losing its light, then that is your sign to get more of GOD in you.

Do not let your lamp go out. The more we pray and meditate on the Lord, the better we become. We have to stay grounded. Do you see a building and say, "Oh, that is a beautiful place? I wonder what it took to get it done like that?"

Some of us question how long it took to get it done. If you are anything like me, I look at each and every detail that was put into it. Anything that has been built requires time, as well as people helping to get the building process done.

One of the first things that is needed is measurement to see exactly how much material will be needed for each room or space. This includes windows, walls, offices or whatever is being built.

Let me relate this to how much the Lord will give us. He will give us exactly however much we ask for. There is no limitation to what He will give us. Then there comes the saw. The saw is put in place so that we can take off what is not needed. There is always a need to cut things out that are not needed.

When we are trying to stay grounded in the Lord, sometimes we have to remove some things in our life, so we will not start shifting. If you do feel that you are starting to shift in a negative way, just know that if you serve the same GOD I serve, then he is an unchanging GOD. Hebrews 13:8 states, "Jesus Christ is the same yesterday, today, and forever." He will never not want you to cry out to Him when you are in need.

We are living in a time where there is so much going on and the days are getting by us really fast, however, there is no situation or time frame that the Lord does not have control over. Every day that passes, we wake up and start our day ready for anything that can take place, but do not be moved.

I have planted one seed and I'm not going to stop watering it. Do not let anyone tell you that your flower is no longer good, or your building is falling. That is not so. If GOD is in it, then it has to grow.

We do not serve a GOD that helps you along the way and leaves you be. We serve a GOD that is with us as long as we allow Him to be with us. Do not be moved by anything or anyone who does not speak positivity into your life. Psalms 16:8 says, "I have set the Lord always before me, because he is at my right hand, I shall not be moved." This is my favorite scripture.

Tragedy may strike, your children or family members may act out or against you, your job may fail, or even sickness may come about, but do not be moved.

We can immerse ourselves in the Word so that when things come about, we are not knocked down or pushed to the point of not coming back. Stand tall and look up to GOD at all times. He made us be bold in Him and, through us, He will allow our light to shine.

Psalm 1:1-3

Blessed is the man that walketh not in the counsel of the ungodly, nor standeth in the way of sinners, Nor sitteth in the seat of the scornful. But his delight is in the law of the LORD; And in his law doth he meditates day and night. And he shall be like a tree planted by the rivers of water, that bringeth forth his fruit in his season; His leaf also shall not wither; And whatsoever he doeth shall prosper.

CHAPTER TWENTY

My GOD, My Mechanic

There is a constant battle going on in the inside of each one of us. Once the Lord has forgiven you, it is time that you forgive yourself. We can be so hard on ourselves about sins from the past. We can sin and bring things upon ourselves and not even know it. In that case, I sinned a lot. I am not proud of it, but I don't mind saying to the Lord that, "Yes, I have fallen short of your glory, but I want to continue to please you at all costs."

Have you ever hurt someone else in the midst of your pain, but you never realized it because you thought that there was nothing wrong with what you did? Your internal pain could affect others around you, especially when they see that you are suffering, but you refuse to get the help that you need. You have said to yourself, over and over, that you will let the Lord deliver you from your own pain and sin, but you still need to be fixed down on the inside.

It all starts with the core. The core is the center of us. Some people want to start fixing themselves from the outside in, but it does not work like that at all. The mind and the heart are connected.

The scripture in Ephesians 2:8-10 states that the mind and the heart must both be engaged in this process, because to have faith in GOD, we must believe and trust GOD, Believing requires the mind, but to trust in one requires the heart.

If your outside is good, but your heart and mind are no good, then these two do not mix. We cannot be two in one. An example of being two in one is a person who has a lot of junk on the inside, but if you were to see the outward appearance, you would want to believe that they are a good person or a person who has no problems.

If you have come through your trials and tribulations of healing, and no longer bring self-infliction upon your own mind and heart, then Praise GOD because He is worthy and He can do it, but it all starts from the inside.

"I need a tune up"

Have you ever looked at life as a ride? I have seen many different aspects of it. I have heard people say, "Jesus take the wheel." You have called the right person if this is who you have called. He is the driver of all our vehicles, but we have to let him drive. I do not care how raggedy you think you are, I know He can fix, repair, and even rebuild you if He needs to. I am a walking testimony.

There were days when I sat and looked at the phone as it rang and could not answer because the inside of me was not right. My heart had become very hard. Can you imagine the ice that causes your pipes to freeze in the winter?

Well, that was me. If He can deliver me, He can do it for you, but it all starts from the heart. Ask the Lord to soften your heart. He will not make an attempt if you do not let Him into your world. It can be really hard when you are battling on the inside, and even if you have your

Christian brothers and sisters around you, it is still up to you if you will allow any change in your life. We need repairs just like an automobile does.

Sometimes, we need a tune-up and that is okay. We are human and the Lord knows that. He knows that we get tired, mentally, physically, and emotionally. He also knows when we are suffering due to tragedy or any situation. He can fix it. There is nothing that is too hard for the GOD that we serve.

Sometimes it is not just a tune-up. We can be going through things and be considered okay but may need some things changed. How long does a car run before it needs the spark plugs changed or the brakes replaced? We operate the same way. Sometimes we just need a little work done on us and there is nothing wrong with that.

Once we get ourselves back in the position and in the place that we need to be in, the next step is how we speak life into ourselves. Yes, the mouth and the tongue are very powerful. How we say things can sometimes determine how we feel. I will refer to our mouths as the motor of the vehicle. The Bible tells us in Proverbs 21:23, "Whoso keepeth his mouth and his tongue keepeth his soul from troubles."

The worst time to speak badly into your life is when you are going through a difficult situation. You could potentially speak negatively into your own destiny. We want to speak life into ourselves and others. We do not want to let that which is dwelling down on the inside come out of us.

If depression and anger is in you, that is exactly what will come out of your mouth. If pain and misery is in you, you will speak those things.

"Hey! How are you doing today?" The response that you give them back is, "I'm not doing too good. I am really depressed." That is not the answer we want to respond with. Instead, we want to say something along the lines of, "I am doing okay, but GOD is keeping me through it all." Your motor is what turns on your car.

Do you understand that your mouth determines how everything else functions? Once you begin to speak, what you say will determine how your heart and mind will operate. We are all built differently, and we all have different outlooks on everything, but one thing that is a fact is the heart, the mind, and the mouth play a really big part in how well you go through your daily life.

There is not one person who does not need a little maintenance done on them. So, if and when you need your repairs just call on GOD. He can make all things new. He is the true Resuscitator of all things big or small.

James 4:8

Draw nigh to God, and he will draw nigh to you. Cleanse your hands, ye sinners; and purify your hearts, ye double minded.

CHAPTER TWENTY-ONE

Stir The Word In You

How much of the Word is in you? We all know that when we go to bake and cook anything there are some ingredients that have to go in with the proper measurements, and they have to be just right.

Have you ever cooked something that was not quite tasteful, but you knew something was missing, so you started thinking to yourself, "What did you forget to put in your recipe?"

I would like to relate these ingredients to us as individuals on the chase for GOD and being in Him. We all run to Christ as we should. We go through turmoil in our lives considering that He is the only one who can help us.

We have our prayer partners and those people who can help us through our everyday situations, but there are times when you have to pray for yourself. So, when we have to pray for ourselves, we must have the correct ingredients in us.

One of the main questions that is asked of Christians is, "What kinds of fruits do we bear?" In other words, "What is inside of us?" Do we have love? Do you love everyone? I mean everyone.

Not just your clique that you are running with or your family and friends, but everyone, no matter their gender or identity. Is there joy down on the inside? What about peace? If we follow the commandments of the Lord, we are granted peace by the Lord Himself.

The scripture of Isaiah 48:17-18 reads, "Thus saith the LORD, thy Redeemer, the Holy One of Israel; I am the LORD thy God which teacheth thee to profit, which leadeth thee by the way that thou shouldest go.18 O that thou hadst hearkened to my commandments!

Then had thy peace been as a river, and thy righteousness as the waves of the sea, and patience." I suffered with patience for a very long time during my healing process, but I knew there was no way that I could be healed or delivered from anything if I did not have any patience for anyone else.

"What ingredients are in you?"

I had to have patience within myself. So, yes, I had to change the ingredients that were inside of me. Do you see yourself helping others or expecting to be healed if there is no kindness in you at all? We, at times, have to get rid of our own trash, clean out our closets, and be restored and renewed with the things that the Lord has for us.

I can assure you that each person He created wants all these qualities to be in them so that they not only can help themselves, but also help others, and that is what it is all about.

When we go into faithfulness and have it down on the inside, there is a priority that takes rank in GOD alone. He should override everything, and His word should be in us. When we immerse ourselves in His word, then that is when we can be ready for war.

My grandmother's pastor would often say "faithfulness" is the criteria to everything. Have you ever gone in for prayer and someone began to pray for you, but you thought about how you have not been in your Word? If we do not have the right measurement of Word in us, then it can be hard to get your prayers through to the Lord.

Have you heard of the phrase in the Bible called "Dead Works?" Our blessings come from our praise and if there is no praise in you, then no blessings come out. There is a song by Shekinah Glory called "Praise Is What I Do." What is it that we are praising?

I am praising GOD and no other, for He is the Author and the Finisher of our lives. We can apply GOD'S Word in our lives by being in the Lord and being filled with the Holy Spirit. John 15:5 states, "I am the vine, you are the branches.

Whoever abides in me and I in him, he it is that bears much fruit, for apart from me you can do nothing." That scripture alone says it all for me. It is so true we are nothing without GOD. If His Word is not in us, we cannot say that we know Him.

We may know of Him, but how well do we really know Him? Increase your ingredients and stir up the many great qualities in you that the Lord gives to us all. When and if you are faced with anything, you will have enough Word in you to get through it all.

Prior to many things in my life, I did not have all of the GOD-like qualities. So, it was hard for me to get through certain storms. I encourage you on this day and hour, while you are reading this book alone, to set up a time of the day to pray and only focus on His Word.

Remember there is a vast number of blessings, and there is also the same amount of pain that can be poured into each of us. Your Word is the best weapon you can have. Take all the greatness that is in the handbook, the best book of life, and apply it to your life.

How well will you apply your ingredients in your life? Consider yourself making the best part of you, which is the GOD in you. Let the Lord stand up in you and shine bright so that everyone can identify the greatness in your life.

1 Peter 5:7

casting all your care upon him; for he careth for you.

CHAPTER TWENTY--TWO

Layers Removed

There are so many layers that we have that become a part of our lives as we travel through this journey of life. We obtain many different emotions from the time we are first exposed to the world. Layers of good times and layers of bad ones as well.

Let me use an example of a person who has had so much grief and pain in their life, however, they still have the desire to please the Lord and do His will. We can have so many gifts that are down on the inside, but the reality is we need more than a gift to operate in the spiritual realm.

I knew that I could in no way win

souls or bring anyone close to the Lord if I did not first seek the Lord myself and know His ways and follow them. Trials and tribulations will break you down, but with the Lord all of it has a purpose. I feel that the Lord allows any tragedy or circumstance in order to get us back to where He wants us or where He would like for us to be in general.

We all have a purpose here to serve in the Lord's kingdom. We cannot make it in with anything extra than what he has designed for us. I will be the first to stand and say that due to the shedding of many tears in certain periods of my life, I had so much covering me that it had begun to weigh me down. Each layer had to be removed one by one.

It is not always easy, especially if you have a view of the world and not of a spiritual mindset.

Although your soul can call out for the Lord, what is it that may be holding you back from the greatest of your gifts? We want to share our treasures with others who have been through struggles in their lives.

I have a firm belief that the Lord intentionally places obstacles for us to not only come out stronger and wiser, but to also birth great things in each one of us. My pain was great. It was something that I would not want anyone to experience, yet I had to come to the realization that there was no way to fulfill or please the Lord if I had not accepted the plan He had for me.

We will never see the plan when it is first introduced to us. The Lord may take you in different directions. We are too busy looking at the whys and what's, and that is normal, but don't dwell on it for too long because it could very well delay your journey. I spent many nights awake during my storm feeling that I would never be able to help anyone or anybody. I thought nothing could ever be better for me.

I had an older lady approach me at one of my physician appointments and when she walked up to me, she said, "Young Lady, can I speak with you for a little bit?" and of course I said, "Sure." She said, "Do you believe that the Lord is allowing you to go through everything that you are going through to not come out strong?

"I have to get rid of the extra."

You have to remove all the layers, set your own problems aside, and be an assistance to someone else." I said, "How can I help anyone in the condition that I am in?" She *said, "Just trust **GOD**. You will find yourself helping someone and healing yourself in the process."*

I went home and laid across the bed. I still was not in total agreement with what was spoken to me. The Lord will use people to encourage others when it is most needed. This was the part of my life where I was in pain, but my healing and deliverance came from assisting others who were headed down the same path as me.

I always had a desire to chase after the Lord and I was leaning toward my Word more when my life changed forever, but he saw something in me that I did not quite see myself. I never thought that I would be in the position to help other people, not after all that I had endured.

I want everyone to know that we are all in a position to help someone else, but there are some things that have to be done first before that can happen.

1 John 3:17 states, "But Whoso hath this world's goods, and seeth his brother have need, and shutteth up his bowels of compassion from him, how dwelleth the love of God in him?" You have to care about your brothers and sisters.

I had an issue with this, and it was not because I did not care for them as individuals. It was because I thought that my issues were bigger than anyone else's issues and this is selfish in the sight of GOD. The Lord expects us to hold one another up in times of need.

When the Lord ministers to your heart, you, in return, should be ready to lift up your brothers and sisters in Christ. It should never be a case where if you don't know them personally, that you should turn your back on them, or treat them as if they are not a concern to you. When you begin to do this, you will be elevating yourself spiritually as well. Did it ever occur to you that when you reach out to your brother or sister, that they very well could be of service to you? You will not know this if you do not complete your assignment in the Lord.

James 5:16 reads, "Confess your faults one to another, and pray one for another, that ye may be healed. The effectual fervent prayer of a righteous man availeth much." We can always use a prayer partner. When two or more come together in Jesus' name, it will come to pass. Little by little, the layers that were covering the best of you will eventually be lifted.

Be free in Jesus' name and keep

walking in it. Everything that the devil tried to tie you down with is gone. The Lord does not want us to be bound. He wants us to be free from bondage and the layers of pain. Walk and do not look back. The weight is lifted. The breakthrough is here. As long as you keep our Great GOD in the midst of everything, there will be blessings on top of blessings in store for you.

If you are reading this and you felt like you could not move forward because of the layers of pain, worries, and any emotion that is not of GOD, understand He has you and you no longer have to bear it alone. Walk in your storms and don't be concerned about being defeated. The Lord will be there every step of the way.

Jeremiah 29:11

For I know the thoughts that I think toward you, saith the LORD, thoughts of peace, and not of evil, to give you an expected end.

CHAPTER TWENTY - THREE

Make Me, Mold Me

We all have come to a point in our lives where we can sit back and reflect on how things used to be, or what they could have been. I think one of the worst things we can do is ponder on the what ifs. I believe that everything that we have been through in this life was set up to be exactly that way. I didn't want to accept that at all.

I wanted to make my own plans and do my own thing, but again it is not up to me. We were created, stripped, molded, and made over in the vision of the Lord only.

As children, we used to talk about

what we wanted our lives to look like, from our dream houses to our dream cars. Does that sound familiar to you? We want to pick how we want our lives to look, and live the way that we want to live, but I do have news for you. The Lord will continue to take us through some things in this life, the good, the bad, the ugly, and the sad, but we have to deal with that which we are dealt.

If someone would have told me that I would go through life and would experience so much loss, I would have told them, "No, that is not what GOD has for me at all." I will say that I feel like I have been taken back a few times, set back, and broken into many pieces.

I was sitting, speaking with one of my grief counselors and she said, "Melissa, tell me how you really feel." I said, "Well, I will tell you this, I feel like a vase that has been broken, and little by little the Lord is putting me back together again."

Her next question was, "Do you consider this vase to be glass or clay?" I responded back to her, and I said, "Well, I would like to consider my vase to be of clay because once glass is broken, you cannot ever repair it to what it used to be. But with the clay, He can just keep on molding me into who He needs me to be and more."

The Lord did not design us to be stagnant and to be in one place. He intends for us to go through the storms of life no matter the size, so that we can grow and be greater in Him. I am not standing on the top of any hill screaming that I am happy about anything that I have endured. However, what I will say is now that I have been through some rough patches, I am more than a conqueror and anything that I have been through, I know the Lord has carried me through.

> "Shake me, break me, rebuild me."

I now know that I will never be the same person again in some aspects, but I will be better in the areas that the Lord needs me to prosper in.

If he called me to do a certain work in Him, then that is what I will do. It is my reasonable service to do what I am called to do. The scripture of Romans 12:1 reads, "I beseech you therefore, brethren, by the mercies of God, that ye present your bodies a living sacrifice, holy and acceptable unto GOD, which is your reasonable service."

What do you think about this scripture? The Lord placed us all here on this earth for a reason, to serve him, and in doing so, to do it in His way, which is holy and acceptable. I cannot be the vessel that He needs me to be if I am repeatedly doing things my way.

So, doing this is part of the process of the Lord making us over into the new creatures that He needs us to be. During our trials and tribulations, whether big or small, He expects for us to come out stronger than ever with a defined purpose that is planned for us individually.

I believe that everyone who is on a move for GOD and His plans will have to face something in their lives. My mirror in looking back shows that everything has had its place and time with me leading up to ministry for the Lord. Isaiah 64:8 states, "But now, Lord, you are our father, We are the clay, and you are our potter. All of us are the work of your hand." We are to be a continuous work in the Lord, but only through Him alone.

I will continue to say, "Lord as you use me for your glory, as I would not be any good for the world's desires, but only for the works of the Lord." I have come a long way, but only because of His grace and mercy. If you are reading this, will you allow the Lord to mold you and make you over?

I am a new creature in the Lord, and I plan to do great things in His name. He gave me the name and I will give Him the reputation as His daughter.

Isaiah 54:17

No weapon that is formed against thee shall prosper; and every tongue that shall rise against thee in judgment thou shalt condemn. This is the heritage of the servants of the LORD, and their righteousness is of me, saith the LORD.

THE FINAL CHAPTER

Keeping the Enemy Away

I was aware of my transition in the Lord that there were, and have been, things consistently trying to take me back to where I used to be spiritually. Once you are broken and being put back together by GOD, then you have to pray more than anything. The type of praying that I am referring to is praying without ceasing.

The more I felt myself becoming the person that the Lord designed me to be, the more the devil tried to find his way back into my life *by reminding me of how I used to feel. I can hear my grandmother in my ear saying, "You better speak to that thing, and it will flee." She is speaking of the devil. If you are reading this, then you know exactly what I am saying.*

The devil wants you to be broken and to stay broken. This is why you have to not allow him to creep in, distract your spirit, or tear you down. I like to stay in my spiritual realm even though I am waking up every day in the natural. I do this by praying as soon as my feet hit the floor. "I did not come this far to be set back in any way," is what I have to keep reminding myself.

Just when you think that you are in the clear, that devil steps back in before you even can begin to plan your day. The devil is there lurking, seeing what he can do to make you bend. I will tell you this, it is okay to talk to yourself. Some people will say that an individual is crazy when they talk to themselves, but I say it is absolutely vital that you do speak to yourself.

*The beginning of your day can be the end of your day if you are not careful about not keeping **GOD** in the beginning, center, and all around you. You can be spirit filled and prayed up, and the minute you walk out the door to work, your past struggles can and will come back up and hinder your whole day from going forth. It is just that easy.*

The days when I felt like I could in no way face the world are gone. I now walk with pride and an understanding that God will be by my side.

I can do all things. The

scripture in Philippians 4:13 reads, "I can do all things through Christ which strengthened me." Do I believe that? Yes, I do. There is no way that I have even gotten this far in life without believing that. If you know that you have been broken and you are better than where you used to be, create a plan if you need to and follow it.

I call it "the survival rules." The first rule is prayer. Prayer changes all and GOD knows all. I refuse to be empty again. When I feel like I am getting low on my spiritual walk, then I need to get into position and get ready for battle. I have never seen a battle lost, but our great GOD needs to know that we are ready to go to war.

When we are preparing for war, all we have to do is believe. If the Lord does not feel that you are prepared to depend on him wholeheartedly, then he will back away until you do. I know, so I am sharing my experiences with you. The enemy will try to taunt you and have you stepping out on your own if you do not allow the Lord to lead you when you are battling with many things.

This battle is not ours but the Lord's. I don't know about you, but this gives me relief. I don't have to wait on an entourage of people to come to my rescue or call up different people when I know who to go to first. We are supposed to have a prayer partner or someone that we can go to, but do not underestimate the power of GOD. It is the Lord alone who restores, rehabilitates, and keeps the life in us going.

I went through a really bad phase in my life after overcoming the many giants that I struggled with, and I just could not pick myself up and go. I had to sit down and do some self-evaluation. The source of my issues had to be cut out so that I could then deal with why it even kept coming back up in my life. This was not always easy for me, but the seeds that were once planted seemed to be growing all over again.

"Eyes wide open"

There is one question that came to mind when I realized this was taking place, and the response that was spoken back to my spirit was, "Melissa you have given up on me." I went into a panic, and I tried to make myself believe that I did not just hear what the Lord had spoken to me.

The tears had begun to fall, and I was so outdone because after the

Lord had shown me who He was, I then turned around and did not carry His promises in my heart. I felt defeated once again. Once I had taken some time out to see exactly what it was that I needed to do to get back to where I needed to be, I confessed with my mouth where I had fallen short.

I feel confession is personal and between you and the Lord (or in this case me and the Lord). Anytime you want to move ahead and get a clean slate, you have to first identify what causes the devil to attack over and over again in the same situations.

Are you ready to continue to walk in all your pain, knowing that the Lord will carry you? As long as you are working with the Lord, then you have succeeded.

I do not know about anyone

else, but I choose to walk in it, no matter what it looks or feels like.

All days will not be good days, however, if GOD is in it, then you are winning. Our lives can be run just like anything that needs refueling. Like a car, when your oil is running low, be ready to refill.

We all have to replace the petroleum that we have burned off when driving from Point A to Point B. Well, we too have to be renewed in Christ from time to time to make sure that we can continue on with the Christian race.

Philippians 3:14 states, "I press toward the mark for the prize of the high calling of GOD in Christ Jesus." I did not get into this Christian race to not make it. Do you choose to walk as well? Don't allow the enemy to keep you in his territory

IN LOVING MEMORY OF

JOYCE MARIE JENKINS

MAKAYLA ALAUNA LANIER

LATASHA TIFFANY COLLINS

DENITA LASHAWN RICE

BRYSON JOSEPH LAVELL RICE

JOSEPH "BO" MCNAIR

ANDREA RENEE HARLEY

Acknowledgement's

TIKEYIA JENKINS

SONIA PETERSON

NICKAYLA WIGGINS

AMBER BENNETT

THE AUTHOR THANKS YOU

www.ingramcontent.com/pod-product-compliance
Lightning Source LLC
Chambersburg PA
CBHW071159160426
43196CB00011B/2126